Contents

Space

Space has always been of interest to people, because our life is also connected with it. The discoveries of space and its exploration are so exciting that one wants to learn more and more new things. Space is the most discussed topic today. The secrets of space never cease to amaze the eyes of people.

Space means empty space in the Universe, which is outside the planetary atmospheres. It contains particles of hydrogen, oxygen and dust, although their concentration is very low and is only a few molecules per cubic meter Also, in some parts of the interstellar medium, electromagnetic radiation and cosmic rays can be encountered. The latter are atoms of nuclei and elementary particles moving at high speed.

The Sun

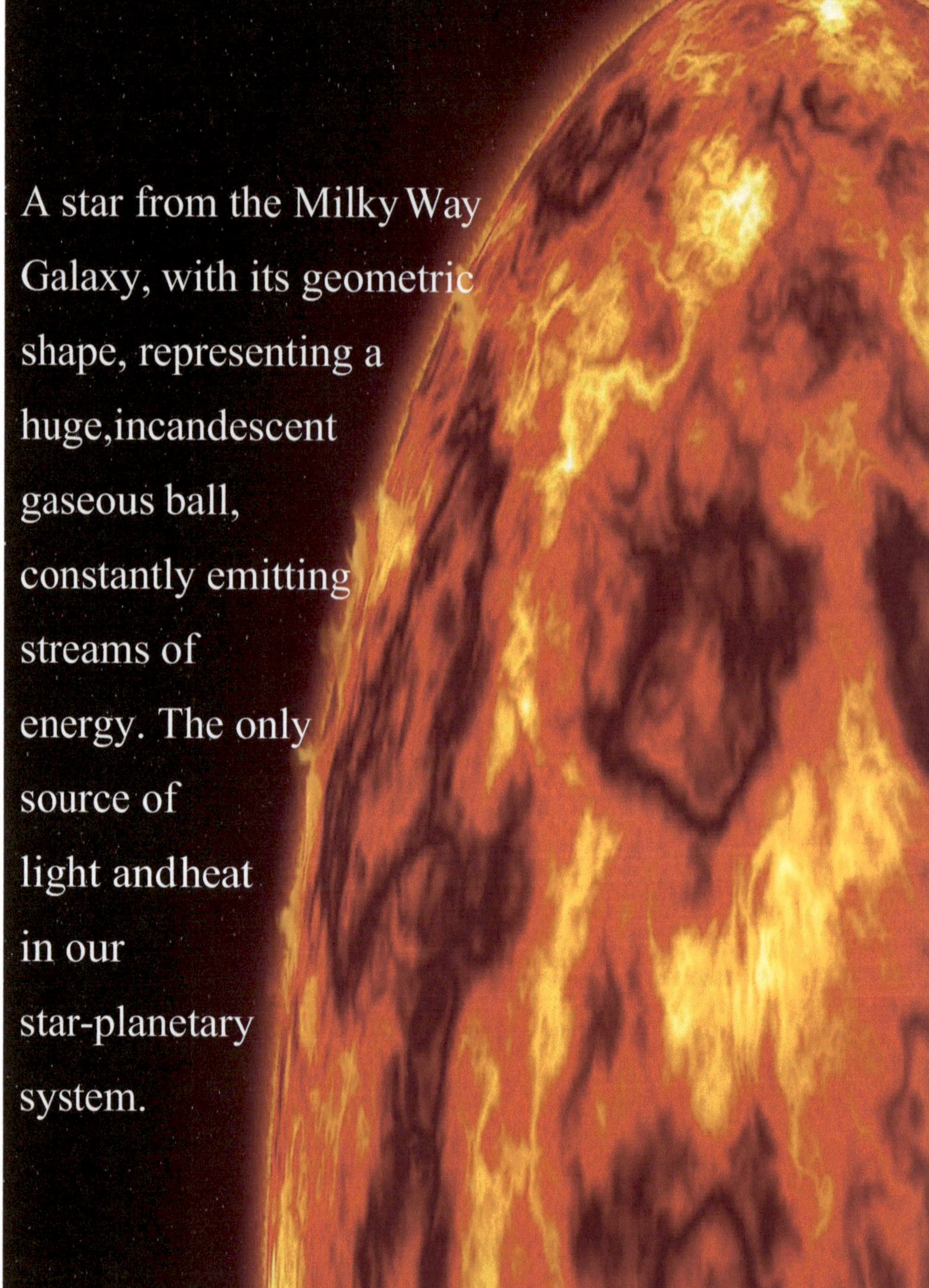

A star from the Milky Way Galaxy, with its geometric shape, representing a huge,incandescent gaseous ball, constantly emitting streams of energy. The only source of light andheat in our star-planetary system.

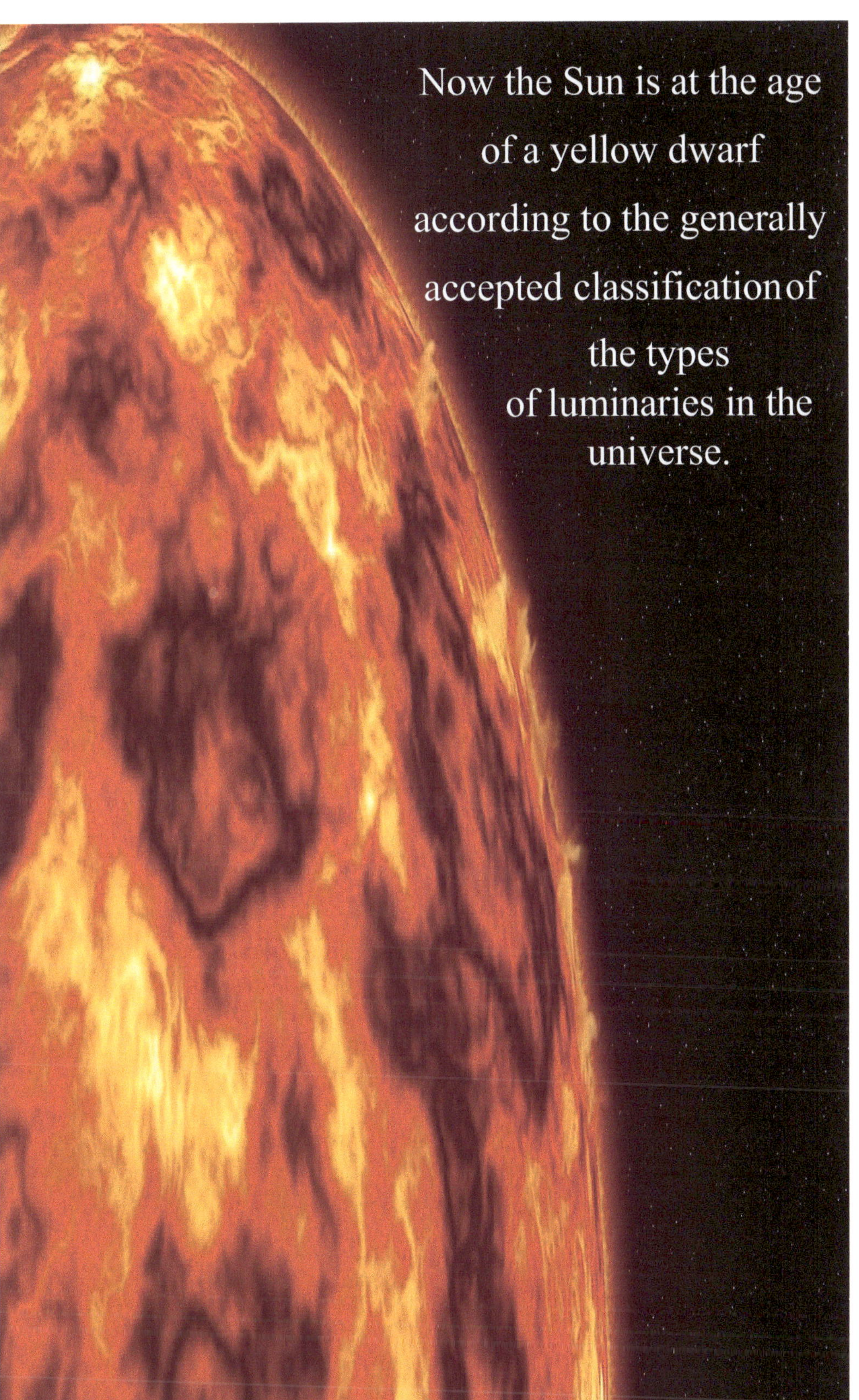

Now the Sun is at the age
of a yellow dwarf
according to the generally
accepted classification of
the types
of luminaries in the
universe.

Apparently, the Sun owes its appearance to the protostars of previous generations, since it contains a significant amount of metals. Its age is 4.5 -4.75 billion years, and all this time it increases its brightness and temperature (flares up).

An interesting fact: the magnetic field of our star has a cycle of change approximately equal to 22 Earth years. Which is equal to two periods of solar activity in 11 years

Such a physical process cannot proceed without loss of mass of hydrogen, which is the main element in the composition of the luminary.

Our solar system

The solar system is a collection of planets orbiting a central star. Scientists managed to establish that it is about 4.57 billion years old, and it appeared due to the gravitational compression of a gas and dust cloud. The system is based on a bright star - the Sun, which holds the planets and other objects. causing them to orbit at a certain distance. It is many times larger than other objects in its area of attraction in diameter.

The solar system is an aggregate consisting of a central star - the Sun and celestial bodies revolving around it.
The solar system includes:
- The Sun (the only star in the solar system);
- 8 planets (including Earth)
- 415 satellites
- tens or hundreds of thousands of various small bodies (comets, meteoric bodies, cosmic dust, etc.).

An interesting fact: the sun has such a large mass that all other planets in the system make up only 0.0014% of its weight.
In the solar system, in addition to the star, there are eight main planets, as well as five dwarf planets. It is located in the Milky Way galaxy, in the Orion arm.

The Inner Plannets

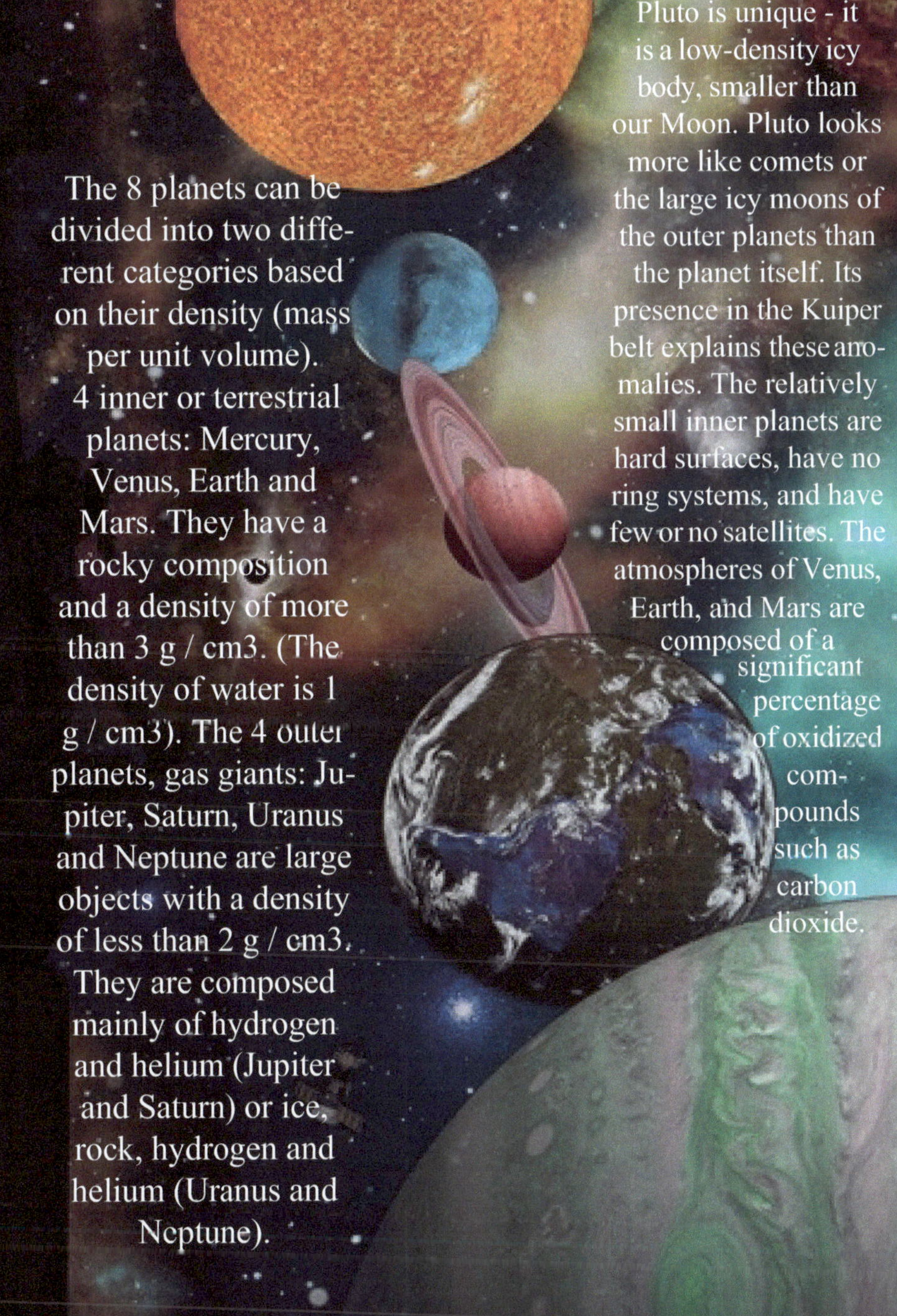

The 8 planets can be divided into two diffe-rent categories based on their density (mass per unit volume). 4 inner or terrestrial planets: Mercury, Venus, Earth and Mars. They have a rocky composition and a density of more than 3 g / cm3. (The density of water is 1 g / cm3). The 4 outer planets, gas giants: Jupiter, Saturn, Uranus and Neptune are large objects with a density of less than 2 g / cm3. They are composed mainly of hydrogen and helium (Jupiter and Saturn) or ice, rock, hydrogen and helium (Uranus and Neptune).

The dwarf planet Pluto is unique - it is a low-density icy body, smaller than our Moon. Pluto looks more like comets or the large icy moons of the outer planets than the planet itself. Its presence in the Kuiper belt explains these ano-malies. The relatively small inner planets are hard surfaces, have no ring systems, and have few or no satellites. The atmospheres of Venus, Earth, and Mars are composed of a significant percentage of oxidized com-pounds such as carbon dioxide.

Among the inner planets, only the Earth has a strong magnetic field that protects it from a hostile environment.

The 4 giant outer planets are much more massive than the terrestrial planets and have a huge atmosphere composed mainly of hydrogen and helium. However, they do not have a solid surface, and their density is so low that one of them, Saturn, would actually float in water.

Each of the outer planets has a magnetic field, a ring system, and many known satellites. Pluto has no known rings and only 5 known moons. Several other Kuiper belt objects and some asteroids also have their own moons. Most of the known satellites move around their planets in the same direction as the planets around the Sun.

They are very diverse, representing a wide range of environments. Io's moon orbits Jupiter and has intense volcanism on its surface.

The largest moon of Saturn, Titan is larger than the planet Mercury

Triton moves in a retrograde orbit around Neptune, that is, in the opposite direction from the planet's orbit around the Sun. The temperature on the satellite's surface is only -236 ° C.

EARTH

The third planet from the Sun, the only one with large territorial areas filled with water. Due to favorable climatic conditions and sufficient resources, it is the only source of life in the solar system.
The radius of the planet is 6378 km.
The homeland of humanity. The distance from it to the Sun ranges from 147 to 152 million km.

The average value of this value is 149.6 million km and is used in astronomy as a unit of measurement for distances - an astronomical unit (AU). The average radius of the Earth is 6371 km, and the mass of our planet is estimated at 5.97 x 1024 kg. The Earth is distinguished from the terrestrial planets by the presence of a very large satellite - the Moon, with a radius of 1737 km.

-The rotation slows down gradually For earthlings, the whole process of slowing down the rotation of the axis occurs almost imperceptibly - 17 milliseconds per 100 years. But the nature of speed is not uniform. For this reason, there is an increase in the length of the day. In day.In140 million years, a day will last 25 hours.

-Earth was believed to be the center of the universe Ancient scientists could observe celestial objects from the position of our planet, so it seemed that all objects in the sky were moving relative to us, and we stayed at one given moment.

As a result, Copernicus stated that the Sun (the
heliocentric system of the world) is at the center of
everything, although now we know that this does not
correspond to reality, if we take the scale of the Universe.
With a strong magnetic field Earth's
magnetic field is created by a
a rapidly rotating nickel-iron
planetary node.

Gas Giants

The plans in our Solar system are divided into internal and external. Those that are located closest to the star have earth-type planets. They are filled with silicate minerals and metal. But behind the fourth acteroidal belt they live their oppo nents - gas giants.
There are four of them, and they also have their own differences. With the start-up of the probes, we were able to study them better and learn a lot of interesting information.
A gas giant is called a planet made of hydrogen and helium. The first name was used by James Blish in 1952. He was a fantastical pictorial and this term does not quite correspond to reality, because the elements in gas giants are transformed into liquid or solid at depth.
In gas giants, a smaller concentration of metal and silicates in the core is observed.

There are 5 different types, based on the scheme of David Sudapka:

I - ammonia clouds. The planes are included here, located in the external area of the system (beyond the ice line). This is the distance where the flying stuff is condensed into solid ice grains.

II - water clouds. They have average temperature indicators (-23 ° C), therefore, too hot for the creation of an ammonia cloudy bed. Booda reflects more strongly, since they are endowed with a higher index of albedo.

III - cloudless. The temperature rises to 80 ° C-530 ° C, therefore, they are devoid of cloudy cover (there is no sufficient amount of chemical substances). They have a low albedo and seem to be floating deep balls, since the methane absorbs the red wavelengths.

IV - alkaline metals. They are heated above 627 ° C, due to which in the atmosphere it starts to domine carbon monoxide. The package also contains the number of alkaline metals. These objects have hot Jupiters.

V - silicate clouds. These are the most heated giants (over 1100 ° C). At the top of the atmospheric layer, silicate and iron cloud formations are arranged. Will look red in the TV view.

Dwarf Planets

The term dwarf planet officially appeared in 2006, when, after the orbit of Neptun, the planets in size with Pluto and large ones were found. From that moment, many bodies in the Solar System are called dwarf planets. In addition, the concept caused a lot of controversy, especially regarding the status and nature of Pluto. Now the MAC is announcing the existence of 5 little planets, and about two hundred are waiting for confirmation. Let's take a look at how the characteristics of the macro planets look like.

A dwarf planet is a celestial object that:

* grows around the sun ;
* has sufficient mass to become almost round ;
* cannot clear its orbital path.

If it is short, then it has any object with a planetary mass, but not a protruding planet or moon. But the body must rotate around the Sun and have a spherical shape.

Below is a list of planets, where their characteristics, description and photos are
i ndicated.

Moons

Move further away from the city fire on a dark night and love the lovely moonlight. The moon is the only earthly satellite that rotates around the earth for more than 3 billion. summer. In other words, the Moon accompanies humanity from the moment of its manifestation. Due to the brightness and accessibility in direct observation, the satellite was reflected in many myths and cultures. Some thought it was God, while others tried to use it to predict events. Let's take a close look at   the interesting facts about the Moon.

The Moon repeats the Earth and also promotes its inner and outer cores, mantle and crust. The core is a solid iron sphere extending over 240 km. The area is not a coherently external core made of liquid iron (300 km). Further, it goes to half-flat layer (500 km). It is believed that it was formed due to the crystallization of the global magma ocean 4.5 billion rubles. summer ago. This process has created a mantia with magnesium and iron. Also in the mantle it is possible to find magmatic rocks, where the iron is larger than ours. Kopa is 50 km away

The core contains only
20% of the total object and
contains not only
metal iron, but also a small
amount of sulfur and nickel.
You can see what the
structure of the moon looks
like on the diagram.

Scientists managed to
confirm the presence of
water on the satellite,
a large part of which is
averagely present at the
pole in the darkened
frontal formations of the
front and back
windows. They think
that it appeared because
of the contact of the
satellite with the sunny
wind.
Lunar geology pauses
with the earth.

The satellite is deprived of a dense atmospheric layer, therefore, there is no weather and wind erosion on it. Small size and low gravity lead to fast cooling and lack of tectonic activity. It is possible to mark a large number of craters and volcanoes. Everywhere there are mountains, mountains, hills and depressions. Stronger than all, the contrast between bright and dark themes is noted. The first ones have lunar heights, and the dark ones - the sea. The heats were formed by magmatic species, pre- sented with field spat and traces of magnesium, pyroxene, iron, olivine, magnetite, and ilm.

Basalt breed is the main reason. Often these areas coincide with the lowlands. You can mark the channels. They are arcuate and linear. These are lava tubes, cooled and dispersed from the moment of volcanic hibernation.

An interesting feature is the lunar domes, created by the emission of lava into the ventilation holes. They have gentle slopes and a diameter of 8-12 km. Mops appeared due to the compression of tectonic plates. Most of them are met on the basis of mopey.

A noteworthy feature of our satellite is shock craters, which are formed when large space stones are dropped. Kinetic shock energy generates a shock wave that leads to depression, because of which a lot of material is pulled out. Maters run from small pits up to 2500 km and a depth of 13 km (Aytken).

Some of the big ones appeared in the early history, after which they started to bend. It is possible to find about 300000 depressions with a width of 1 km. In addition, the moon soil is of interest. It was formed because of the blows of acteroids and some billions of years ago.

Stages of space exploration

For the first time, progressive mankind believed in the reality of flight to distant worlds at the end of the 19th century. It was then that it became clear that if the aircraft was given the speed necessary to overcome gravity and kept for a sufficient time, it would be able to go beyond the Earth's atmosphere and gain a foothold

in orbit, like the Moon, revolving around the Earth. The problem was in the engines.

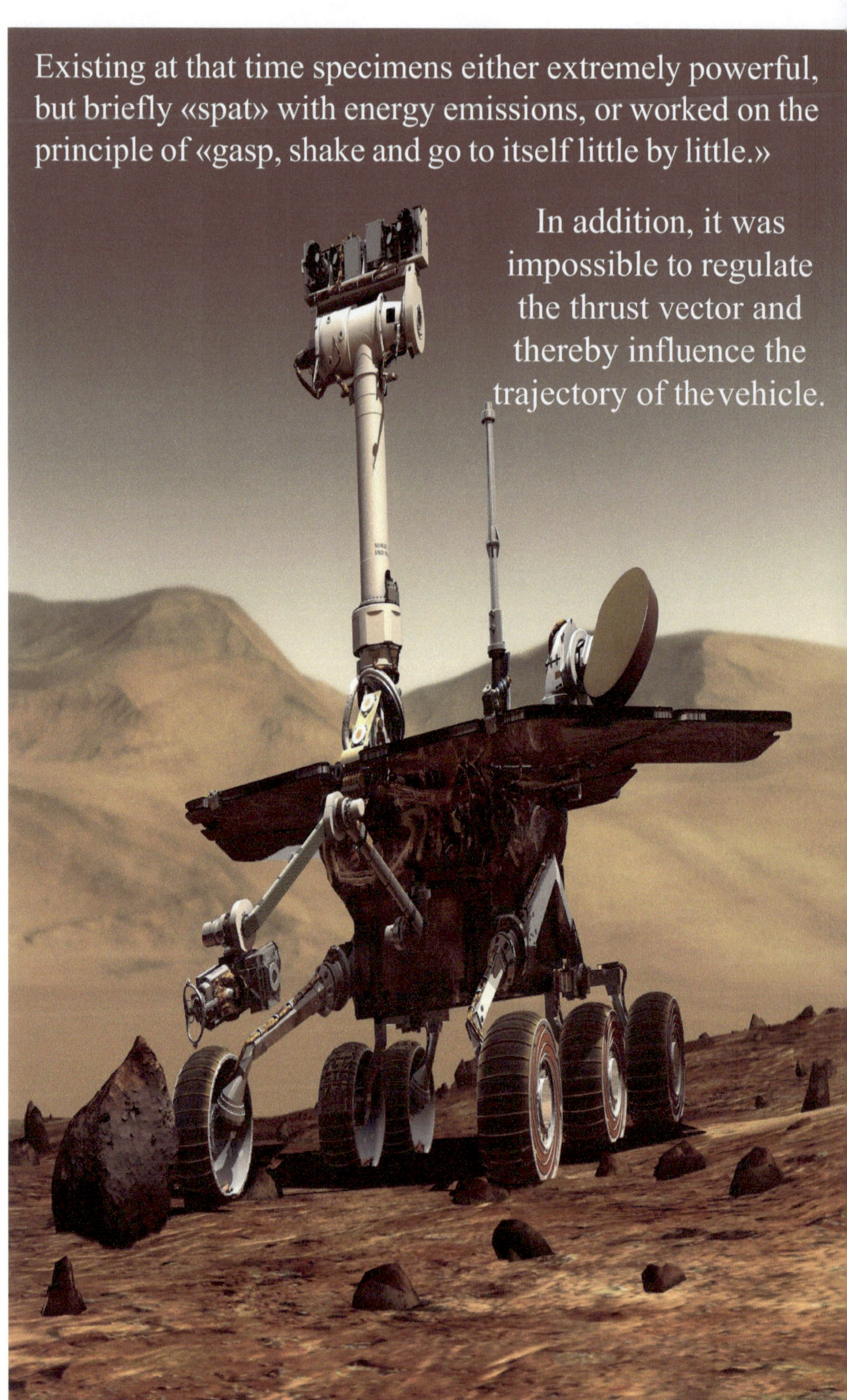
Existing at that time specimens either extremely powerful, but briefly «spat» with energy emissions, or worked on the principle of «gasp, shake and go to itself little by little.»

In addition, it was impossible to regulate the thrust vector and thereby influence the trajectory of the vehicle.

Finally, at the beginning of the 20th century, researchers drew attention to the rocket engine, the principle of operation of which has been known to mankind since the turn of our era: the fuel burns in the rocket body, simultaneously lightening its mass, and the released energy moves the rocket forward

The first rocket capable of launching an object beyond gravity was designed by Tsiolkovsky in 1903.

Stage I - the first launch of the spacecraft

The date when space exploration began is October 4, 1957 - this is the day when the Soviet Union, as part of its space program, was the first to launch a spacecraft into space - Sputnik-1. On this day, a spherical satellite entered orbit, transmitting back a signal of a successful launch.

It was launched into orbit using the R-7 rocket, designed under the direction of Sergei Korolev. The silhouette of the R-7, the progenitor of all subsequent space rockets, is still recognizable in the ultra-modern Soyuz launch vehicle, which successfully sends into orbit «trucks» and «cars» with astronauts and tourists on board - the same four «legs» of the packet scheme and red nozzles.

It completed a full orbit around the Earth in 96 minutes. The «star life» of the iron pioneer of astronautics lasted three months, but during this period he covered a fantastic path of 60 million km! It was so popular that in the Soviet Union even Christmas decorations and badges were made in its uniform.

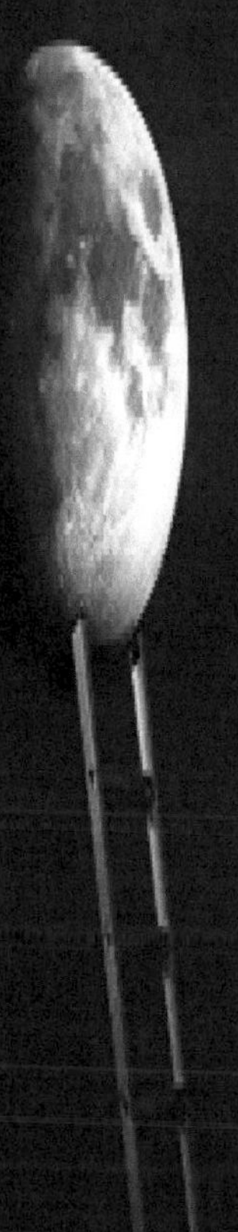

The exploration of outer space by the USSR put an end to the efforts of the Americans to be the first to conquer space. The sole purpose of its launch was to test theories. In the end, space exploration in the 50-60s ceased to seem a ghostly task. It also sparked a huge amount of science fiction that flooded the pages of books and TV screens.

Stage II - the first living beings in orbit

The success of the first launch inspired
the designers, and the prospect of sending
a living creature into space and retur-
ning it safe and sound no longer seemed
impossible. Just a month after the launch of
Sputnik-1 the first animal, the dog Laika

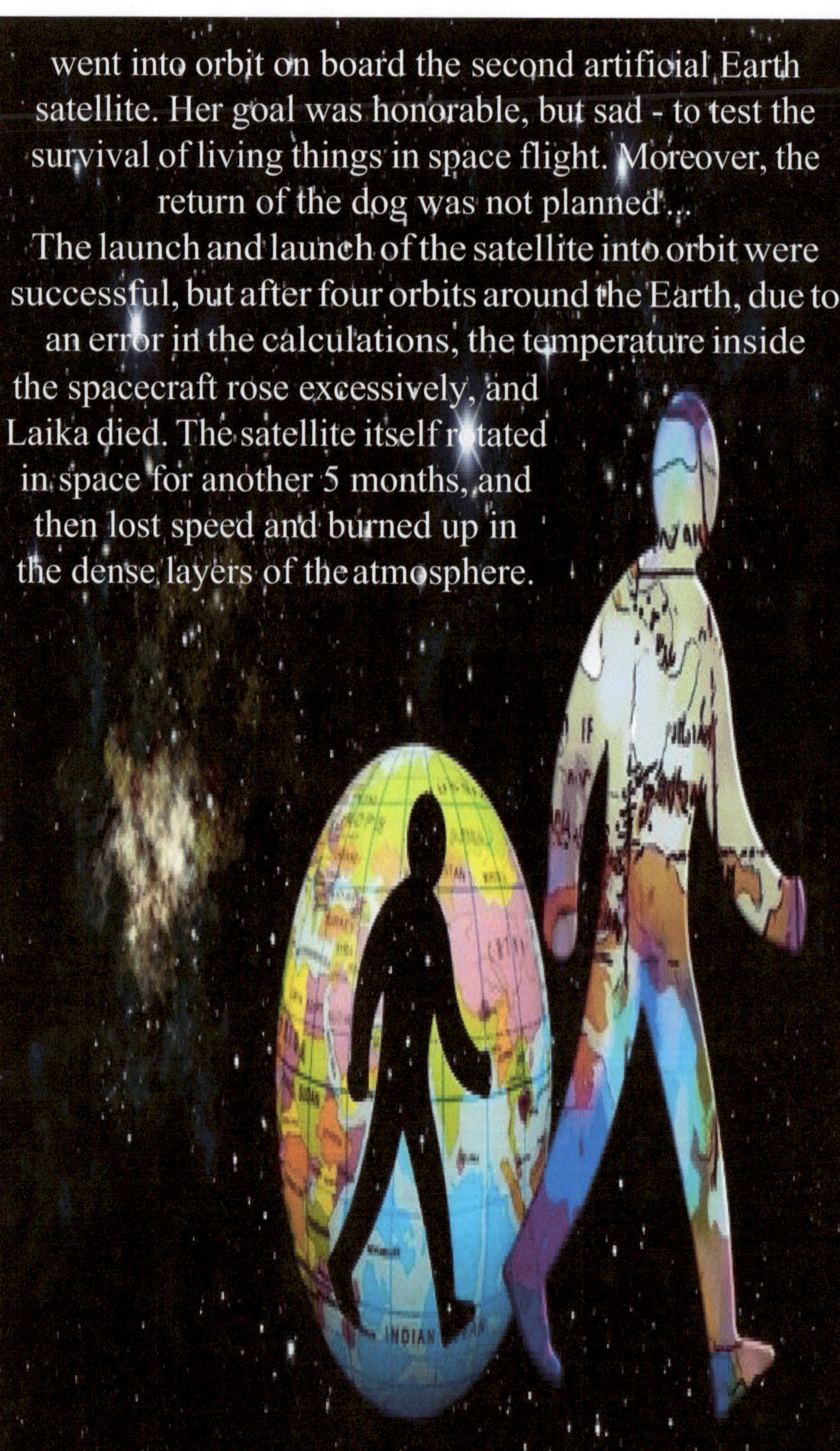

went into orbit on board the second artificial Earth satellite. Her goal was honorable, but sad - to test the survival of living things in space flight. Moreover, the return of the dog was not planned...
The launch and launch of the satellite into orbit were successful, but after four orbits around the Earth, due to an error in the calculations, the temperature inside the spacecraft rose excessively, and Laika died. The satellite itself rotated in space for another 5 months, and then lost speed and burned up in the dense layers of the atmosphere.

The first shaggy cosmonauts who, upon their return, greeted their «senders» with joyful barking, were Belka and Strelka, who set off to conquer the heavens on the fifth satellite in August 1960.

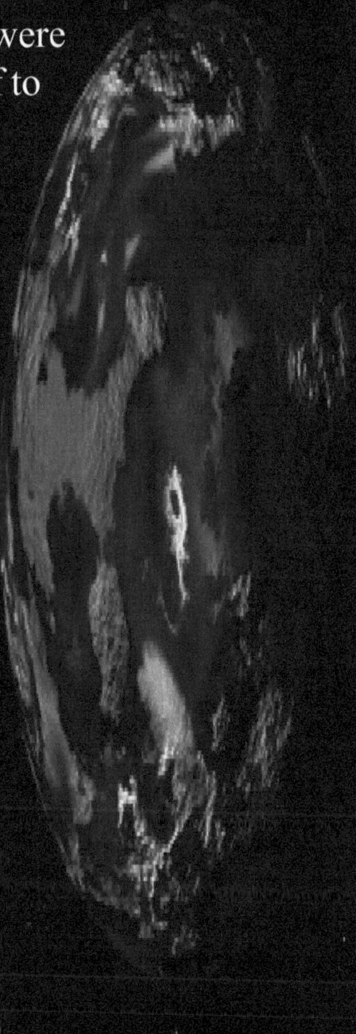

Their flight lasted just over a day, and during this time the dogs managed to fly around the planet 17 times. All this time, they were watched from monitors in the Flight Control Center - by the way, it was because of the contrast that white dogs were chosen - after all, the image was then black and white.

As a result of the launch, the spacecraft itself was also finalized and finally approved - in just 8 months the first man will go into space in a similar vehicle.

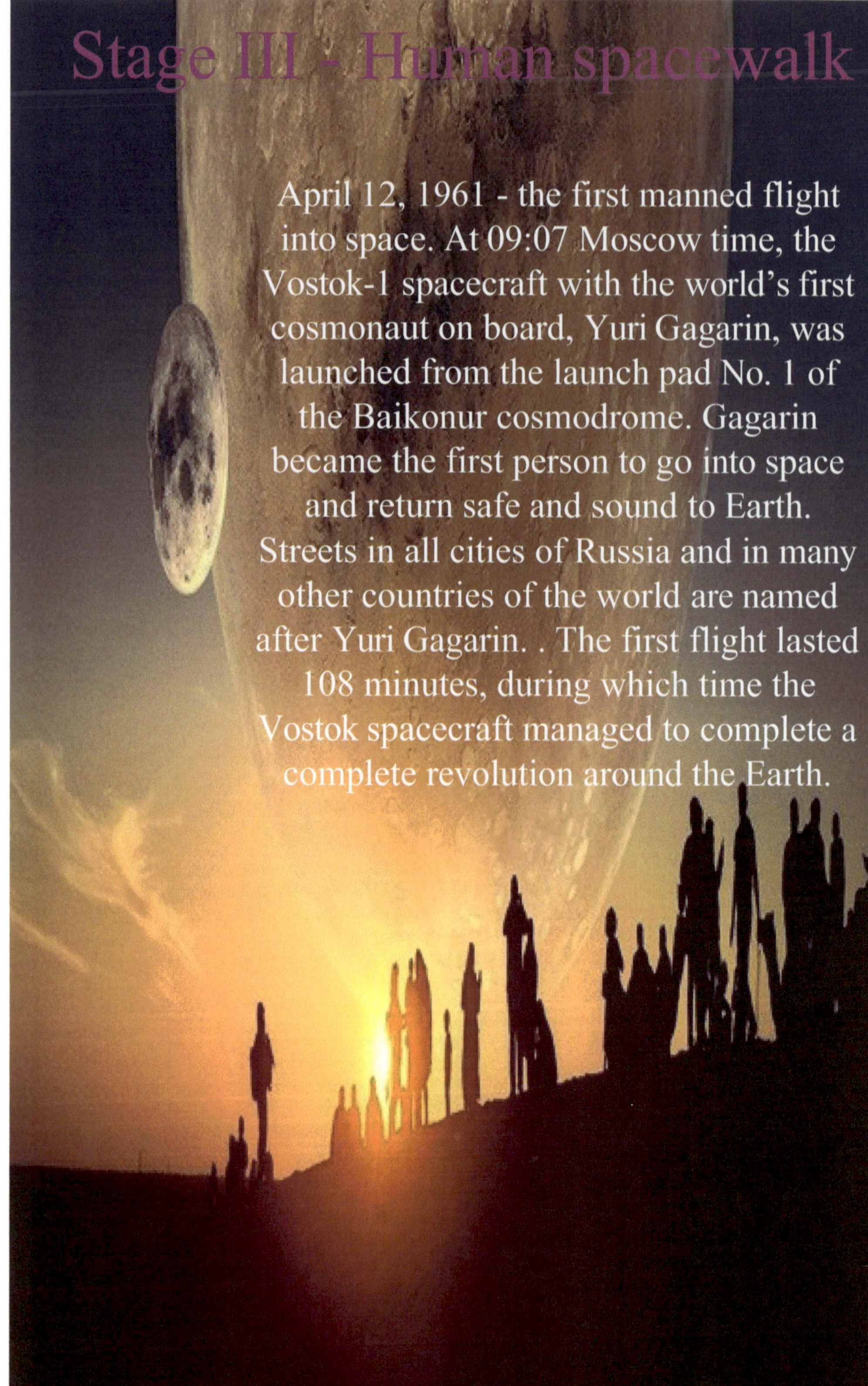

Stage III - Human spacewalk

April 12, 1961 - the first manned flight into space. At 09:07 Moscow time, the Vostok-1 spacecraft with the world's first cosmonaut on board, Yuri Gagarin, was launched from the launch pad No. 1 of the Baikonur cosmodrome. Gagarin became the first person to go into space and return safe and sound to Earth. Streets in all cities of Russia and in many other countries of the world are named after Yuri Gagarin. . The first flight lasted 108 minutes, during which time the Vostok spacecraft managed to complete a complete revolution around the Earth.

During the flight, many basic tests were carried out: for the first time a person drank, ate, took notes and performed simple mathematical calculations in space. Before that, no one knew how a person would actually feel in orbit.

Stage IV - the first landing on the moon

Although the Soviet Union was the first to go into space and even the first to launch a person into Earth's orbit, the United States was the first whose astronauts were able to successfully land on the nearest space body from Earth - on the Moon satellite.

On July 24, 1969, two Apollo 11 crew members stepped onto the lunar surface: Neil Armstrong and Buzz Aldrin made one exit and stayed on the Earth satellite for two and a half hours.

Then the famous phrase was said in the news: «This is a small step for man, but a huge leap for all mankind.» Armstrong not only managed to visit the surface of the moon, but also to bring soil samples to Earth.
In total, from 1969 to 1972, 6 flights with a landing on the moon were performed under the Apollo program. Over the years, 12 people have visited the satellite.

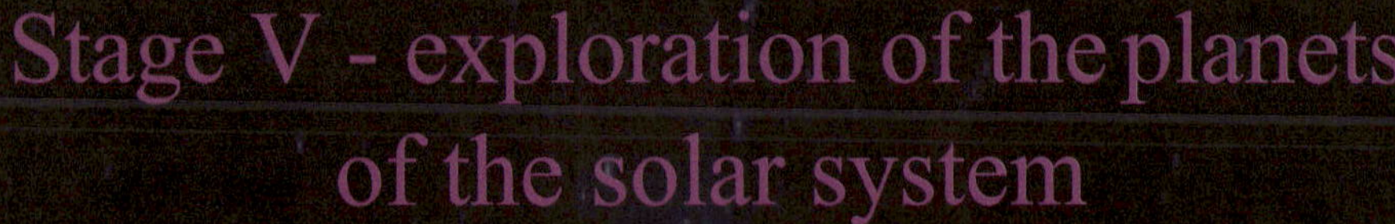

Stage V - exploration of the planets of the solar system

Mars

The Soviet Marsexploration program began in 1964, with the most significant results achieved by 1971. The automated interplanetary station «Mars-2» became the first artificial object on the surface of the Red Planet, although the device suffered an accident.

Following on the heels of «Mars-3» in the same year made a soft landing for thefirst time in history. The communication session lasted only 14 seconds - during this time the first photo was transmitted from the planet's surface.

Venus

Another Soviet program, but for the study of Venus; again, many major achievements and discoveries. Soviet devices found out that the nearest neighbor has incredibly high pressure and is not a twin of the Earth. In 1970, Venera 7 made the first ever soft landing, and five years later, Venera 9 transmitted the first photographs from the surface.

Unofficially, Venus was considered a «Soviet» planet, as the Union made great efforts to study it, leaving Mars to competitors.

Viking

In 1975, two identical vehicles, Viking-1 and Viking-2, were sent to Mars in order to find traces of life in the ground. Life was not found, but a soft landing was made, the first soil samples and the first panoramic color photos from the surface were obtained. The devices were supposed to work for 90 days, but they significantly exceeded this period. Viking 1, for example, remained functional for 5 years.

Voyager

Voyager (or Traveler) is a NASA project to explore the distant planets of the solar system - Jupiter, Saturn, Neptune, Uranus and Pluto (which was then still considered a planet), as well as their satellites. Voyager 1 and Voyager 2 were launched in 1977.

For the first time they transmitted detailed color images of distant planets and for the first time photographed the largest satellites.

Stage VI - humanity goes beyond the solar system

In 1972, a spacecraft called Pioneer 10 was launched, which, passing near Saturn, traveled beyond the solar system. And although «Pioneer-10» did not report anything new about the world outside our system, it became proof that mankind is capable of entering other systems. in 1977, Voyager 1, after studying Jupiter and Saturn, embarked on an additional mission to explore remote regions of the solar system, including the Kuiper belt and the heliosphere boundary.

Voyager 1 «is the fastest of the spacecraft leaving the solar system, as well as the most distant from the Earth object that has been created by man.

A case with a gold plate is fixed on board the device, where the location of the Earth is indicated for the alleged aliens, as well as a number of images and sounds are recorded.

VII stage - the beginning of the international comprehensive space exploration

Launch of the reusable spacecraft Columbia

Launch of the Mir space station.

In 1981, NASA launched a reusable spacecraft called Columbia, which has been in service for more than twenty years and makes almost thirty journeys into outer space, providing incredibly useful information about it to humans. Shuttle Columbia retires in 2003 and makes way for newer spacecraft.

In 1986, the Soviet Union launched the base unit of the Mir station into near-earth orbit. The station itself, without exaggeration, has become a symbol of the era. For more than 12 years, the Mir station had a permanent «population»: Valery Polyakov spent 437 days on the Mir - and this is a record of a man's stay in space. 23,000 experiments were carried out and a huge amount of data on interplanetary space was obtained.

Launch of the Hubble Telescope

The Hubble Telescope , launched in 1990 , has become the «eyes» of humanity. The orbiting telescope was able to look as far as no one before, and show such beauties of the universe, which no one could imagine.

The International Space Station came to replace Mir in 1998 at. The ISS is almost 5 times larger than its predecessor and serves as a space «summer residence» for mankind to this day. One of the main goals in the creation of the station is the possibility of carrying out various experiments and experiments that require the presence of unique conditions of space, and in particular - weightlessness, as well as vacuum and microgravity.

The International Space Station came to replace Mir in 1998 at. The ISS is almost 5 times larger than its predecessor and serves as a space «summer residence» for mankind to this day. One of the main goals in the creation of the station is the possibility of carrying out various experiments and experiments that require the presence of unique conditions of space, and in particular - weightlessness, as well as vacuum and microgravity.

IX-stage – intensive exploration and commercialization of space

The beginning of the XXI century is marked by the further intensive conquest of outer space by man. Work and experiments on the ISS continue, images from the Hubble telescope are being studied and analyzed. The discovery of new cosmic phenomena and objects is amazing.
The study of our solar system continues:
•June 24, 2000 - NEAR Shoemaker station became the first artificial satellite of an asteroid (433 Eros).
•une 30, 2004 - Cassini station became the first artificial satellite of Saturn.
•January 15, 2006 - Stardust station delivered samples of Comet Wild 2 to Earth.
•March 17, 2011 - Messenger became the first artificial satellite of Mercury.

New frontiers

The automatic interplanetary station «New Horizons» within the framework of NASA's «New Frontiers» program was launched in 2006. Its goal is to study Pluto and other objects in the Kuiper belt. The Kuiper Belt is a region of the solar system similar to the asteroid belt between Mars and Jupiter, only this belt is located at the far reaches of the solar system and consists of dwarf planets like Pluto. In addition, the «New Horizons» apparatus became the fastest in history.

Chang'e-4

In 2019, the Chinese automatic interplanetary station «Chang'e-4» made a soft landing on the far side of the moon for the first time in history. During the mission, a new communication system was tested, and cotton seeds sprouted for the first time on an Earth satellite. They, along with other crops, were placed in a container designed to test the possibility of forming a closed biosphere.

Commercial space exploration

Humanity cannot imagine itself without space. In addition to all the advantages of practical space exploration, the commercial component is also developing.
Private space companies:
• SpaceX (founded in 2002) and its cosmodrome
• Blue Origin - founded in 2000.
•i rgin Orbit is a company formed by the Virgin Group in 2017. An air launch project is being prepared [1]
• Suborbital SC SpaceShip of Scaled Composites: SpaceShipOne - the world's first private spacecraft; SpaceShipTwo is a tourist suborbital spacecraft, a further development of SpaceShipOne.
• Interstellar Technologies - the first Japanese firm in the field of private astronautics; established in 2003.

• S7 Space is a Russian company whose main activity is launching space rockets and placing space objects into orbit.

www.ingramcontent.com/pod-product-compliance
Lightning Source LLC
Chambersburg PA
CBHW040306240726
48664CB00006B/1396